THIS BOOK BELONGS TO:

CONTACT INFORMATION	
NAME:	
ADDRESS:	
PHONE:	

START / END DATES

___/___/___   TO   ___/___/___

DEDICATION

This Homeschool Hours Journal Log book is dedicated to all the Homeschoolers out there who want to record their students home school hours and document the process.

You are my inspiration for producing books and I'm honored to be a part of keeping all of your Homeschool Hours notes and records organized.

This journal notebook will help you record your details about your child's homeschooling hours.

Thoughtfully put together with these sections to record:
Student Name, Weekly Date, Subject, Start Time, End Time and Notes.

HOW TO USE THIS BOOK

The purpose of this book is to keep all of your Homeschool Hours notes all in one place. It will help keep you organized.

This Homeschool Hours Journal will allow you to accurately document every detail about logging your homeschool hours. It's a great way to chart your course through logging your homeschool hours.

Here are examples of the prompts for you to fill in and write about your experience in this book:

- Student Name - Write your student's name.
- Weekly Date - Log the week of and the year. Undated for your convenience.
- Subject - Record the subject.
- Start Time - For writing the time you start the subject.
- End Time - Log the time you end the subject. Notes - Write any other important information you choose, for example, core learning curriculum, noncore learning, lesson, attendance, special activities, nature walk, tests results, your state laws such as Missouri, what you're planning every day, etc

Enjoy!

HOMESCHOOL HOURS LOG BOOK

STUDENT NAME:		WEEK OF:	

SUBJECT	MONDAY		TUESDAY		WEDNESDAY		THURSDAY		FRIDAY	
	START	END	START	END	START	END	START	END	START	END

NOTES

HOMESCHOOL HOURS LOG BOOK

STUDENT NAME:			WEEK OF:	

SUBJECT	MONDAY		TUESDAY		WEDNESDAY		THURSDAY		FRIDAY	
	START	END	START	END	START	END	START	END	START	END

NOTES

HOMESCHOOL HOURS LOG BOOK

STUDENT NAME:		WEEK OF:	

SUBJECT	MONDAY		TUESDAY		WEDNESDAY		THURSDAY		FRIDAY	
	START	END	START	END	START	END	START	END	START	END

NOTES

HOMESCHOOL HOURS LOG BOOK

STUDENT NAME:		WEEK OF:	

SUBJECT	MONDAY		TUESDAY		WEDNESDAY		THURSDAY		FRIDAY	
	START	END	START	END	START	END	START	END	START	END

NOTES

HOMESCHOOL HOURS LOG BOOK

STUDENT NAME:			WEEK OF:	

SUBJECT	MONDAY		TUESDAY		WEDNESDAY		THURSDAY		FRIDAY	
	START	END	START	END	START	END	START	END	START	END

NOTES

HOMESCHOOL HOURS LOG BOOK

STUDENT NAME:		WEEK OF:	

SUBJECT	MONDAY		TUESDAY		WEDNESDAY		THURSDAY		FRIDAY	
	START	END	START	END	START	END	START	END	START	END

NOTES

HOMESCHOOL HOURS LOG BOOK

STUDENT NAME:		WEEK OF:	

SUBJECT	MONDAY		TUESDAY		WEDNESDAY		THURSDAY		FRIDAY	
	START	END	START	END	START	END	START	END	START	END

NOTES

HOMESCHOOL HOURS LOG BOOK

STUDENT NAME:		WEEK OF:	

SUBJECT	MONDAY		TUESDAY		WEDNESDAY		THURSDAY		FRIDAY	
	START	END	START	END	START	END	START	END	START	END

NOTES

HOMESCHOOL HOURS LOG BOOK

STUDENT NAME: **WEEK OF:**

SUBJECT	MONDAY		TUESDAY		WEDNESDAY		THURSDAY		FRIDAY	
	START	END	START	END	START	END	START	END	START	END

NOTES

HOMESCHOOL HOURS LOG BOOK

STUDENT NAME:			WEEK OF:		

SUBJECT	MONDAY		TUESDAY		WEDNESDAY		THURSDAY		FRIDAY	
	START	END	START	END	START	END	START	END	START	END

NOTES

HOMESCHOOL HOURS LOG BOOK

STUDENT NAME:		WEEK OF:	

SUBJECT	MONDAY		TUESDAY		WEDNESDAY		THURSDAY		FRIDAY	
	START	END	START	END	START	END	START	END	START	END

NOTES

HOMESCHOOL HOURS LOG BOOK

STUDENT NAME:		WEEK OF:	

SUBJECT	MONDAY		TUESDAY		WEDNESDAY		THURSDAY		FRIDAY	
	START	END	START	END	START	END	START	END	START	END

NOTES

HOMESCHOOL HOURS LOG BOOK

STUDENT NAME:		WEEK OF:	

SUBJECT	MONDAY		TUESDAY		WEDNESDAY		THURSDAY		FRIDAY	
	START	END	START	END	START	END	START	END	START	END

NOTES

HOMESCHOOL HOURS LOG BOOK

STUDENT NAME:		WEEK OF:	

SUBJECT	MONDAY		TUESDAY		WEDNESDAY		THURSDAY		FRIDAY	
	START	END	START	END	START	END	START	END	START	END

NOTES

HOMESCHOOL HOURS LOG BOOK

STUDENT NAME:		WEEK OF:	

SUBJECT	MONDAY		TUESDAY		WEDNESDAY		THURSDAY		FRIDAY	
	START	END	START	END	START	END	START	END	START	END

NOTES

HOMESCHOOL HOURS LOG BOOK

STUDENT NAME:		WEEK OF:	

SUBJECT	MONDAY		TUESDAY		WEDNESDAY		THURSDAY		FRIDAY	
	START	END	START	END	START	END	START	END	START	END

NOTES

HOMESCHOOL HOURS LOG BOOK

STUDENT NAME:			WEEK OF:	

SUBJECT	MONDAY		TUESDAY		WEDNESDAY		THURSDAY		FRIDAY	
	START	END	START	END	START	END	START	END	START	END

NOTES

HOMESCHOOL HOURS LOG BOOK

STUDENT NAME:	WEEK OF:

SUBJECT	MONDAY		TUESDAY		WEDNESDAY		THURSDAY		FRIDAY	
	START	END	START	END	START	END	START	END	START	END

NOTES

HOMESCHOOL HOURS LOG BOOK

STUDENT NAME:			WEEK OF:	

SUBJECT	MONDAY		TUESDAY		WEDNESDAY		THURSDAY		FRIDAY	
	START	END	START	END	START	END	START	END	START	END

NOTES

HOMESCHOOL HOURS LOG BOOK

STUDENT NAME:		WEEK OF:	

SUBJECT	MONDAY		TUESDAY		WEDNESDAY		THURSDAY		FRIDAY	
	START	END	START	END	START	END	START	END	START	END

NOTES

HOMESCHOOL HOURS LOG BOOK

STUDENT NAME:		WEEK OF:	

SUBJECT	MONDAY		TUESDAY		WEDNESDAY		THURSDAY		FRIDAY	
	START	END	START	END	START	END	START	END	START	END

NOTES

HOMESCHOOL HOURS LOG BOOK

STUDENT NAME:		WEEK OF:	

SUBJECT	MONDAY		TUESDAY		WEDNESDAY		THURSDAY		FRIDAY	
	START	END	START	END	START	END	START	END	START	END

NOTES

HOMESCHOOL HOURS LOG BOOK

STUDENT NAME: | WEEK OF:

SUBJECT	MONDAY		TUESDAY		WEDNESDAY		THURSDAY		FRIDAY	
	START	END	START	END	START	END	START	END	START	END

NOTES

HOMESCHOOL HOURS LOG BOOK

STUDENT NAME:		WEEK OF:	

SUBJECT	MONDAY		TUESDAY		WEDNESDAY		THURSDAY		FRIDAY	
	START	END	START	END	START	END	START	END	START	END

NOTES

HOMESCHOOL HOURS LOG BOOK

STUDENT NAME:		WEEK OF:

SUBJECT	MONDAY		TUESDAY		WEDNESDAY		THURSDAY		FRIDAY	
	START	END	START	END	START	END	START	END	START	END

NOTES

HOMESCHOOL HOURS LOG BOOK

STUDENT NAME:		WEEK OF:

SUBJECT	MONDAY		TUESDAY		WEDNESDAY		THURSDAY		FRIDAY	
	START	END	START	END	START	END	START	END	START	END

NOTES

HOMESCHOOL HOURS LOG BOOK

STUDENT NAME:		WEEK OF:	

SUBJECT	MONDAY		TUESDAY		WEDNESDAY		THURSDAY		FRIDAY	
	START	END	START	END	START	END	START	END	START	END

NOTES

HOMESCHOOL HOURS LOG BOOK

STUDENT NAME: _____   WEEK OF: _____

SUBJECT	MONDAY		TUESDAY		WEDNESDAY		THURSDAY		FRIDAY	
	START	END	START	END	START	END	START	END	START	END

NOTES

HOMESCHOOL HOURS LOG BOOK

STUDENT NAME: WEEK OF:

SUBJECT	MONDAY		TUESDAY		WEDNESDAY		THURSDAY		FRIDAY	
	START	END	START	END	START	END	START	END	START	END

NOTES

HOMESCHOOL HOURS LOG BOOK

STUDENT NAME: _____ **WEEK OF:** _____

SUBJECT	MONDAY		TUESDAY		WEDNESDAY		THURSDAY		FRIDAY	
	START	END	START	END	START	END	START	END	START	END

NOTES

HOMESCHOOL HOURS LOG BOOK

STUDENT NAME:		WEEK OF:	

SUBJECT	MONDAY		TUESDAY		WEDNESDAY		THURSDAY		FRIDAY	
	START	END	START	END	START	END	START	END	START	END

NOTES

HOMESCHOOL HOURS LOG BOOK

STUDENT NAME:		WEEK OF:	

SUBJECT	MONDAY		TUESDAY		WEDNESDAY		THURSDAY		FRIDAY	
	START	END	START	END	START	END	START	END	START	END

NOTES

HOMESCHOOL HOURS LOG BOOK

STUDENT NAME:		WEEK OF:	

SUBJECT	MONDAY		TUESDAY		WEDNESDAY		THURSDAY		FRIDAY	
	START	END	START	END	START	END	START	END	START	END

NOTES

HOMESCHOOL HOURS LOG BOOK

STUDENT NAME:			WEEK OF:	

SUBJECT	MONDAY		TUESDAY		WEDNESDAY		THURSDAY		FRIDAY	
	START	END	START	END	START	END	START	END	START	END

NOTES

HOMESCHOOL HOURS LOG BOOK

STUDENT NAME: **WEEK OF:**

SUBJECT	MONDAY		TUESDAY		WEDNESDAY		THURSDAY		FRIDAY	
	START	END	START	END	START	END	START	END	START	END

NOTES

HOMESCHOOL HOURS LOG BOOK

STUDENT NAME: WEEK OF:

SUBJECT	MONDAY		TUESDAY		WEDNESDAY		THURSDAY		FRIDAY	
	START	END	START	END	START	END	START	END	START	END

NOTES

HOMESCHOOL HOURS LOG BOOK

STUDENT NAME:		WEEK OF:	

SUBJECT	MONDAY		TUESDAY		WEDNESDAY		THURSDAY		FRIDAY	
	START	END	START	END	START	END	START	END	START	END

NOTES

HOMESCHOOL HOURS LOG BOOK

STUDENT NAME: | | WEEK OF:

SUBJECT	MONDAY		TUESDAY		WEDNESDAY		THURSDAY		FRIDAY	
	START	END	START	END	START	END	START	END	START	END

NOTES

HOMESCHOOL HOURS LOG BOOK

| STUDENT NAME: | | | | WEEK OF: | | | | | | |

SUBJECT	MONDAY		TUESDAY		WEDNESDAY		THURSDAY		FRIDAY	
	START	END	START	END	START	END	START	END	START	END

NOTES

HOMESCHOOL HOURS LOG BOOK

STUDENT NAME:		WEEK OF:	

SUBJECT	MONDAY		TUESDAY		WEDNESDAY		THURSDAY		FRIDAY	
	START	END	START	END	START	END	START	END	START	END

NOTES

HOMESCHOOL HOURS LOG BOOK

STUDENT NAME:		WEEK OF:	

SUBJECT	MONDAY		TUESDAY		WEDNESDAY		THURSDAY		FRIDAY	
	START	END	START	END	START	END	START	END	START	END

NOTES

HOMESCHOOL HOURS LOG BOOK

STUDENT NAME:		WEEK OF:	

SUBJECT	MONDAY		TUESDAY		WEDNESDAY		THURSDAY		FRIDAY	
	START	END	START	END	START	END	START	END	START	END

NOTES

HOMESCHOOL HOURS LOG BOOK

| STUDENT NAME: | | WEEK OF: | |

SUBJECT	MONDAY		TUESDAY		WEDNESDAY		THURSDAY		FRIDAY	
	START	END	START	END	START	END	START	END	START	END

NOTES

HOMESCHOOL HOURS LOG BOOK

STUDENT NAME:		WEEK OF:	

SUBJECT	MONDAY		TUESDAY		WEDNESDAY		THURSDAY		FRIDAY	
	START	END	START	END	START	END	START	END	START	END

NOTES

HOMESCHOOL HOURS LOG BOOK

STUDENT NAME:		WEEK OF:	

SUBJECT	MONDAY		TUESDAY		WEDNESDAY		THURSDAY		FRIDAY	
	START	END	START	END	START	END	START	END	START	END

NOTES

HOMESCHOOL HOURS LOG BOOK

STUDENT NAME:		WEEK OF:	

SUBJECT	MONDAY		TUESDAY		WEDNESDAY		THURSDAY		FRIDAY	
	START	END	START	END	START	END	START	END	START	END

NOTES

HOMESCHOOL HOURS LOG BOOK

STUDENT NAME:		WEEK OF:	

SUBJECT	MONDAY		TUESDAY		WEDNESDAY		THURSDAY		FRIDAY	
	START	END	START	END	START	END	START	END	START	END

NOTES

HOMESCHOOL HOURS LOG BOOK

STUDENT NAME:		WEEK OF:	

SUBJECT	MONDAY		TUESDAY		WEDNESDAY		THURSDAY		FRIDAY	
	START	END	START	END	START	END	START	END	START	END

NOTES

HOMESCHOOL HOURS LOG BOOK

| STUDENT NAME: | | | | | | | | | | | WEEK OF: | |

SUBJECT	MONDAY		TUESDAY		WEDNESDAY		THURSDAY		FRIDAY	
	START	END	START	END	START	END	START	END	START	END

NOTES

HOMESCHOOL HOURS LOG BOOK

STUDENT NAME:		WEEK OF:	

SUBJECT	MONDAY		TUESDAY		WEDNESDAY		THURSDAY		FRIDAY	
	START	END	START	END	START	END	START	END	START	END

NOTES

HOMESCHOOL HOURS LOG BOOK

STUDENT NAME:		WEEK OF:	

SUBJECT	MONDAY		TUESDAY		WEDNESDAY		THURSDAY		FRIDAY	
	START	END	START	END	START	END	START	END	START	END

NOTES

HOMESCHOOL HOURS LOG BOOK

STUDENT NAME:		WEEK OF:	

SUBJECT	MONDAY		TUESDAY		WEDNESDAY		THURSDAY		FRIDAY	
	START	END	START	END	START	END	START	END	START	END

NOTES

HOMESCHOOL HOURS LOG BOOK

STUDENT NAME: WEEK OF:

SUBJECT	MONDAY		TUESDAY		WEDNESDAY		THURSDAY		FRIDAY	
	START	END	START	END	START	END	START	END	START	END

NOTES

HOMESCHOOL HOURS LOG BOOK

STUDENT NAME:			WEEK OF:	

SUBJECT	MONDAY		TUESDAY		WEDNESDAY		THURSDAY		FRIDAY	
	START	END	START	END	START	END	START	END	START	END

NOTES

HOMESCHOOL HOURS LOG BOOK

| STUDENT NAME: | | | | WEEK OF: | | | |

SUBJECT	MONDAY		TUESDAY		WEDNESDAY		THURSDAY		FRIDAY	
	START	END	START	END	START	END	START	END	START	END

NOTES

HOMESCHOOL HOURS LOG BOOK

STUDENT NAME:		WEEK OF:	

SUBJECT	MONDAY		TUESDAY		WEDNESDAY		THURSDAY		FRIDAY	
	START	END	START	END	START	END	START	END	START	END

NOTES

HOMESCHOOL HOURS LOG BOOK

STUDENT NAME: | WEEK OF:

SUBJECT	MONDAY		TUESDAY		WEDNESDAY		THURSDAY		FRIDAY	
	START	END	START	END	START	END	START	END	START	END

NOTES

HOMESCHOOL HOURS LOG BOOK

STUDENT NAME:		WEEK OF:	

SUBJECT	MONDAY		TUESDAY		WEDNESDAY		THURSDAY		FRIDAY	
	START	END	START	END	START	END	START	END	START	END

NOTES

HOMESCHOOL HOURS LOG BOOK

STUDENT NAME:		WEEK OF:	

SUBJECT	MONDAY		TUESDAY		WEDNESDAY		THURSDAY		FRIDAY	
	START	END	START	END	START	END	START	END	START	END

NOTES

HOMESCHOOL HOURS LOG BOOK

STUDENT NAME:		WEEK OF:	

SUBJECT	MONDAY		TUESDAY		WEDNESDAY		THURSDAY		FRIDAY	
	START	END	START	END	START	END	START	END	START	END

NOTES

HOMESCHOOL HOURS LOG BOOK

STUDENT NAME:		WEEK OF:	

SUBJECT	MONDAY		TUESDAY		WEDNESDAY		THURSDAY		FRIDAY	
	START	END	START	END	START	END	START	END	START	END

NOTES

HOMESCHOOL HOURS LOG BOOK

STUDENT NAME:		WEEK OF:	

SUBJECT	MONDAY		TUESDAY		WEDNESDAY		THURSDAY		FRIDAY	
	START	END	START	END	START	END	START	END	START	END

NOTES

HOMESCHOOL HOURS LOG BOOK

STUDENT NAME:		WEEK OF:	

SUBJECT	MONDAY		TUESDAY		WEDNESDAY		THURSDAY		FRIDAY	
	START	END	START	END	START	END	START	END	START	END

NOTES

HOMESCHOOL HOURS LOG BOOK

STUDENT NAME: **WEEK OF:**

SUBJECT	MONDAY		TUESDAY		WEDNESDAY		THURSDAY		FRIDAY	
	START	END	START	END	START	END	START	END	START	END

NOTES

HOMESCHOOL HOURS LOG BOOK

STUDENT NAME:	WEEK OF:

SUBJECT	MONDAY		TUESDAY		WEDNESDAY		THURSDAY		FRIDAY	
	START	END	START	END	START	END	START	END	START	END

NOTES

HOMESCHOOL HOURS LOG BOOK

STUDENT NAME:		WEEK OF:	

SUBJECT	MONDAY		TUESDAY		WEDNESDAY		THURSDAY		FRIDAY	
	START	END	START	END	START	END	START	END	START	END

NOTES

HOMESCHOOL HOURS LOG BOOK

STUDENT NAME: WEEK OF:

SUBJECT	MONDAY		TUESDAY		WEDNESDAY		THURSDAY		FRIDAY	
	START	END	START	END	START	END	START	END	START	END

NOTES

HOMESCHOOL HOURS LOG BOOK

STUDENT NAME:		WEEK OF:

SUBJECT	MONDAY		TUESDAY		WEDNESDAY		THURSDAY		FRIDAY	
	START	END	START	END	START	END	START	END	START	END

NOTES

HOMESCHOOL HOURS LOG BOOK

STUDENT NAME:		WEEK OF:	

SUBJECT	MONDAY		TUESDAY		WEDNESDAY		THURSDAY		FRIDAY	
	START	END	START	END	START	END	START	END	START	END

NOTES

HOMESCHOOL HOURS LOG BOOK

STUDENT NAME:		WEEK OF:

SUBJECT	MONDAY		TUESDAY		WEDNESDAY		THURSDAY		FRIDAY	
	START	END	START	END	START	END	START	END	START	END

NOTES

HOMESCHOOL HOURS LOG BOOK

STUDENT NAME:		WEEK OF:	

SUBJECT	MONDAY		TUESDAY		WEDNESDAY		THURSDAY		FRIDAY	
	START	END	START	END	START	END	START	END	START	END

NOTES

HOMESCHOOL HOURS LOG BOOK

STUDENT NAME: **WEEK OF:**

SUBJECT	MONDAY		TUESDAY		WEDNESDAY		THURSDAY		FRIDAY	
	START	END	START	END	START	END	START	END	START	END

NOTES

HOMESCHOOL HOURS LOG BOOK

STUDENT NAME:		WEEK OF:	

SUBJECT	MONDAY		TUESDAY		WEDNESDAY		THURSDAY		FRIDAY	
	START	END	START	END	START	END	START	END	START	END

NOTES

HOMESCHOOL HOURS LOG BOOK

STUDENT NAME:		WEEK OF:	

SUBJECT	MONDAY		TUESDAY		WEDNESDAY		THURSDAY		FRIDAY	
	START	END	START	END	START	END	START	END	START	END

NOTES

HOMESCHOOL HOURS LOG BOOK

STUDENT NAME:		WEEK OF:	

SUBJECT	MONDAY		TUESDAY		WEDNESDAY		THURSDAY		FRIDAY	
	START	END	START	END	START	END	START	END	START	END

NOTES

HOMESCHOOL HOURS LOG BOOK

STUDENT NAME:		WEEK OF:

SUBJECT	MONDAY		TUESDAY		WEDNESDAY		THURSDAY		FRIDAY	
	START	END	START	END	START	END	START	END	START	END

NOTES

HOMESCHOOL HOURS LOG BOOK

STUDENT NAME:		WEEK OF:

SUBJECT	MONDAY		TUESDAY		WEDNESDAY		THURSDAY		FRIDAY	
	START	END	START	END	START	END	START	END	START	END

NOTES

HOMESCHOOL HOURS LOG BOOK

| STUDENT NAME: | | | | | | | | | | | WEEK OF: |

SUBJECT	MONDAY		TUESDAY		WEDNESDAY		THURSDAY		FRIDAY	
	START	END	START	END	START	END	START	END	START	END

NOTES

HOMESCHOOL HOURS LOG BOOK

STUDENT NAME:				WEEK OF:	

SUBJECT	MONDAY		TUESDAY		WEDNESDAY		THURSDAY		FRIDAY	
	START	END	START	END	START	END	START	END	START	END

NOTES

HOMESCHOOL HOURS LOG BOOK

STUDENT NAME:		WEEK OF:	

SUBJECT	MONDAY		TUESDAY		WEDNESDAY		THURSDAY		FRIDAY	
	START	END	START	END	START	END	START	END	START	END

NOTES

HOMESCHOOL HOURS LOG BOOK

STUDENT NAME:		WEEK OF:	

SUBJECT	MONDAY		TUESDAY		WEDNESDAY		THURSDAY		FRIDAY	
	START	END	START	END	START	END	START	END	START	END

NOTES

HOMESCHOOL HOURS LOG BOOK

STUDENT NAME:		WEEK OF:	

SUBJECT	MONDAY		TUESDAY		WEDNESDAY		THURSDAY		FRIDAY	
	START	END	START	END	START	END	START	END	START	END

NOTES

HOMESCHOOL HOURS LOG BOOK

STUDENT NAME:		WEEK OF:	

SUBJECT	MONDAY		TUESDAY		WEDNESDAY		THURSDAY		FRIDAY	
	START	END	START	END	START	END	START	END	START	END

NOTES

HOMESCHOOL HOURS LOG BOOK

STUDENT NAME:		WEEK OF:	

SUBJECT	MONDAY		TUESDAY		WEDNESDAY		THURSDAY		FRIDAY	
	START	END	START	END	START	END	START	END	START	END

NOTES

HOMESCHOOL HOURS LOG BOOK

| STUDENT NAME: | | WEEK OF: | |

SUBJECT	MONDAY		TUESDAY		WEDNESDAY		THURSDAY		FRIDAY	
	START	END	START	END	START	END	START	END	START	END

NOTES

HOMESCHOOL HOURS LOG BOOK

STUDENT NAME:		WEEK OF:	

SUBJECT	MONDAY		TUESDAY		WEDNESDAY		THURSDAY		FRIDAY	
	START	END	START	END	START	END	START	END	START	END

NOTES

HOMESCHOOL HOURS LOG BOOK

STUDENT NAME: **WEEK OF:**

SUBJECT	MONDAY		TUESDAY		WEDNESDAY		THURSDAY		FRIDAY	
	START	END	START	END	START	END	START	END	START	END

NOTES

HOMESCHOOL HOURS LOG BOOK

STUDENT NAME:		WEEK OF:	

SUBJECT	MONDAY		TUESDAY		WEDNESDAY		THURSDAY		FRIDAY	
	START	END	START	END	START	END	START	END	START	END

NOTES

HOMESCHOOL HOURS LOG BOOK

STUDENT NAME:		WEEK OF:

SUBJECT	MONDAY		TUESDAY		WEDNESDAY		THURSDAY		FRIDAY	
	START	END	START	END	START	END	START	END	START	END

NOTES

HOMESCHOOL HOURS LOG BOOK

STUDENT NAME:		WEEK OF:	

SUBJECT	MONDAY		TUESDAY		WEDNESDAY		THURSDAY		FRIDAY	
	START	END	START	END	START	END	START	END	START	END

NOTES

HOMESCHOOL HOURS LOG BOOK

STUDENT NAME: WEEK OF:

SUBJECT	MONDAY		TUESDAY		WEDNESDAY		THURSDAY		FRIDAY	
	START	END	START	END	START	END	START	END	START	END

NOTES

HOMESCHOOL HOURS LOG BOOK

STUDENT NAME:		WEEK OF:	

SUBJECT	MONDAY		TUESDAY		WEDNESDAY		THURSDAY		FRIDAY	
	START	END	START	END	START	END	START	END	START	END

NOTES

HOMESCHOOL HOURS LOG BOOK

STUDENT NAME:		WEEK OF:	

SUBJECT	MONDAY		TUESDAY		WEDNESDAY		THURSDAY		FRIDAY	
	START	END	START	END	START	END	START	END	START	END

NOTES

HOMESCHOOL HOURS LOG BOOK

STUDENT NAME: | **WEEK OF:**

SUBJECT	MONDAY		TUESDAY		WEDNESDAY		THURSDAY		FRIDAY	
	START	END	START	END	START	END	START	END	START	END

NOTES

HOMESCHOOL HOURS LOG BOOK

| STUDENT NAME: | | WEEK OF: | |

SUBJECT	MONDAY		TUESDAY		WEDNESDAY		THURSDAY		FRIDAY	
	START	END	START	END	START	END	START	END	START	END

NOTES

HOMESCHOOL HOURS LOG BOOK

STUDENT NAME:		WEEK OF:	

SUBJECT	MONDAY		TUESDAY		WEDNESDAY		THURSDAY		FRIDAY	
	START	END	START	END	START	END	START	END	START	END

NOTES

HOMESCHOOL HOURS LOG BOOK

STUDENT NAME:			WEEK OF:		

SUBJECT	MONDAY		TUESDAY		WEDNESDAY		THURSDAY		FRIDAY	
	START	END	START	END	START	END	START	END	START	END

NOTES

HOMESCHOOL HOURS LOG BOOK

| STUDENT NAME: | | | | WEEK OF: | |

SUBJECT	MONDAY		TUESDAY		WEDNESDAY		THURSDAY		FRIDAY	
	START	END	START	END	START	END	START	END	START	END

NOTES

HOMESCHOOL HOURS LOG BOOK

STUDENT NAME:		WEEK OF:	

SUBJECT	MONDAY		TUESDAY		WEDNESDAY		THURSDAY		FRIDAY	
	START	END	START	END	START	END	START	END	START	END

NOTES

HOMESCHOOL HOURS LOG BOOK

STUDENT NAME:					WEEK OF:	

SUBJECT	MONDAY		TUESDAY		WEDNESDAY		THURSDAY		FRIDAY	
	START	END	START	END	START	END	START	END	START	END

NOTES

HOMESCHOOL HOURS LOG BOOK

STUDENT NAME:				WEEK OF:		

SUBJECT	MONDAY		TUESDAY		WEDNESDAY		THURSDAY		FRIDAY	
	START	END	START	END	START	END	START	END	START	END

NOTES

HOMESCHOOL HOURS LOG BOOK

STUDENT NAME: | WEEK OF:

SUBJECT	MONDAY		TUESDAY		WEDNESDAY		THURSDAY		FRIDAY	
	START	END	START	END	START	END	START	END	START	END

NOTES

HOMESCHOOL HOURS LOG BOOK

STUDENT NAME:				WEEK OF:	

SUBJECT	MONDAY		TUESDAY		WEDNESDAY		THURSDAY		FRIDAY	
	START	END	START	END	START	END	START	END	START	END

NOTES

HOMESCHOOL HOURS LOG BOOK

STUDENT NAME:		WEEK OF:	

SUBJECT	MONDAY		TUESDAY		WEDNESDAY		THURSDAY		FRIDAY	
	START	END	START	END	START	END	START	END	START	END

NOTES

HOMESCHOOL HOURS LOG BOOK

| STUDENT NAME: | | | | WEEK OF: | | |

SUBJECT	MONDAY		TUESDAY		WEDNESDAY		THURSDAY		FRIDAY	
	START	END	START	END	START	END	START	END	START	END

NOTES